Piano Made FUN for the Young

Pre-Reading Made FUN

Starter Book

Kevin and Julia Olson

Production: Frank J. Hackinson
Production Coordinators: Peggy Gallagher and Philip Groeber
Editors: Edwin McLean and Peggy Gallagher
Cover and Interior Illustrations: Julia Olson
Engraving: Tempo Music Press, Inc.
Printer: Tempo Music Press, Inc.

THE F·J·H MUSIC COMPANY INC.

Frank J. Hackinson

ISBN-13: 978-1-56939-942-2

Notes to the Teacher and Parent . . .

Piano Made FUN for the Young is an early childhood piano curriculum designed to teach and reinforce the basics of piano study, in a spirit of FUN, PLAYFULNESS, and SUCCESS. The curriculum consists of *Sing-Along Activity Books* with CD's and leveled piano books with CD's. Notes and concepts are taught at a careful and steady pace, giving students a solid foundation without moving too quickly. It is especially effective in a group setting, but great for private students as well.

Young children enjoy lessons that offer a variety of experiences. This curriculum provides diverse learning opportunities that incorporate singing, movement, games, and more. A typical lesson is divided into two areas:

   *Theory Made FUN; Counting Made FUN; Notes Made FUN*

During Rug Time, students sit on the floor near the piano and sing songs using the *Sing-Along Activity Books* to learn and review concepts. Singing the simple songs keeps their attention and helps them have fun while learning. Teachers who are not comfortable singing can use the CD's to listen to the songs with their students. Because the songs are short and easy to remember, many of them can be reviewed in a matter of minutes. **The beginning of each unit in the piano books indicates which concepts to cover at Rug Time.**

   *Pre-Reading Made FUN, Starter Book; Note Reading Made FUN, Book 1*

During Piano Time, students use the leveled piano books with CD's to learn to play and read music at a pace that is steady and comfortable. The music is simple and easy to read so young students do not become frustrated. The themed units and play-along CD's make the learning process fun and interesting. (Each piece on the CD is recorded at a slow practice tempo; students may follow the indicated tempo and dynamic when ready.)

This *Pre-Reading Made FUN, Starter Book* is the first piano book used during Piano Time. It is designed to give young students a solid foundation of early musical concepts and piano topography. The black-key pieces are written as keyboard pictures, making the music intuitive and easy to read. Because the students do not have to think about note values, they can concentrate on hand position and a steady beat. Students can build finger dexterity without the added frustration of note reading and counting. The white keys are introduced through simple improvisational activities that are designed to help the student learn the names of the white keys in an easy and creative way.

We are confident this curriculum will give young students an effective way to get started with the piano, in an atmosphere they can enjoy!

Remember, you can visit **www.PianoMadeFun.com** for free printables and teaching aids.

Kevin and Julia Olson

FJH2162

Practice Time at Home . . .

It is very important for parents to be willing to participate with daily practice time at home. You do not need to spend *much* time, but it is important to spend *some* time each day. Young students need careful supervision when they are first learning new pieces.

Here are a few suggestions for practice time at home:

Start out each practice session with a few songs from the *Sing-Along Activity Books*. (You may wish to use the CD.) Check to see which unit your child's teacher has assigned for the week, and look at the beginning of that unit to find which songs to sing. You do not need to sing every song every day. Try to sing each song at least a few times per week, so your child can become familiar with the concepts. Young children enjoy singing the same songs over and over.

Once you have finished singing a few of the songs, move to the piano to help your child practice the pieces the teacher has assigned in *Pre-Reading Made FUN, Starter Book*. Listen to the song on the CD first, then help your child practice without the CD until they are ready to play with it. Encourage your child to practice each piece slowly and carefully, with nicely curved fingers. You may want to point along in the music as your child practices a new piece. Once he/she is comfortable, you won't need to point any longer.

Remember that young children need consistent reinforcement. You may even find that they sometimes forget something they have already learned. This is normal. Be patient and consistent and your child will eventually learn the pieces. It is also a good idea to consistently review old pieces. Just because your child has moved ahead in the book, does not mean he/she should stop playing the pieces he/she has already learned. This is a good time for your child to play the pieces along with the CD. Young children love to play pieces that are comfortable to them, so go back and review pieces often.

Visit **www.PianoMadeFun.com** for more detailed instructions on how to help your child practice the pieces in this book. You can also go there for supplemental games and activities to do with your child at home.

Teacher Information for Rug Time . . .

The pictures below represent the concepts that will be covered during Rug Time using the *Theory Made FUN Sing-Along Activity Book*. They are listed here for easy reference. It is not meant for students to memorize all of these concepts at once. Students will memorize and retain the information as they sing the songs and review them each week. The beginning of each unit will indicate which concepts to cover for that unit. Visit **www.PianoMadeFun.com** for resources to use at Rug Time.

Piano Day

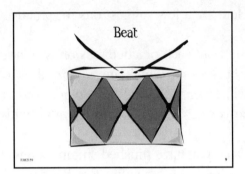
Beat

Tempo

Largo

Andante

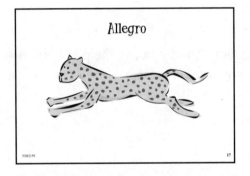
Allegro

p is for Piano

f is for Forte

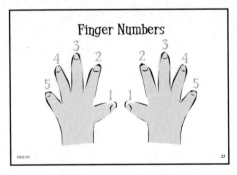
Finger Numbers

Spider Fingers

The Black Keys

The Musical Alphabet

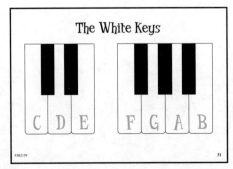
The White Keys

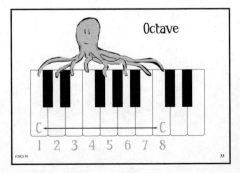
Octave

FJH2162

Table of Contents

UNIT 1

 **Rug Time**

Sit on the floor and sing through the songs in the Theory Made FUN Sing-Along Book tracks 1-11.

Visit **www.PianoMadeFun.com** for fun ideas to go along with this unit.

 **Piano Time**

Right Hand on the 2-Black-Key Group

Place your right hand fingers 2 and 3 on any 2-black-key group on your piano.
Try playing them with nicely curved "spider fingers."

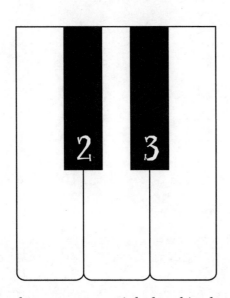
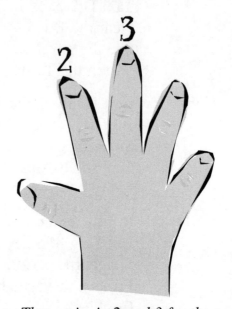

Have your teacher trace your right hand in the space below. Then write in 2 and 3 for the correct fingers.

FJH2162

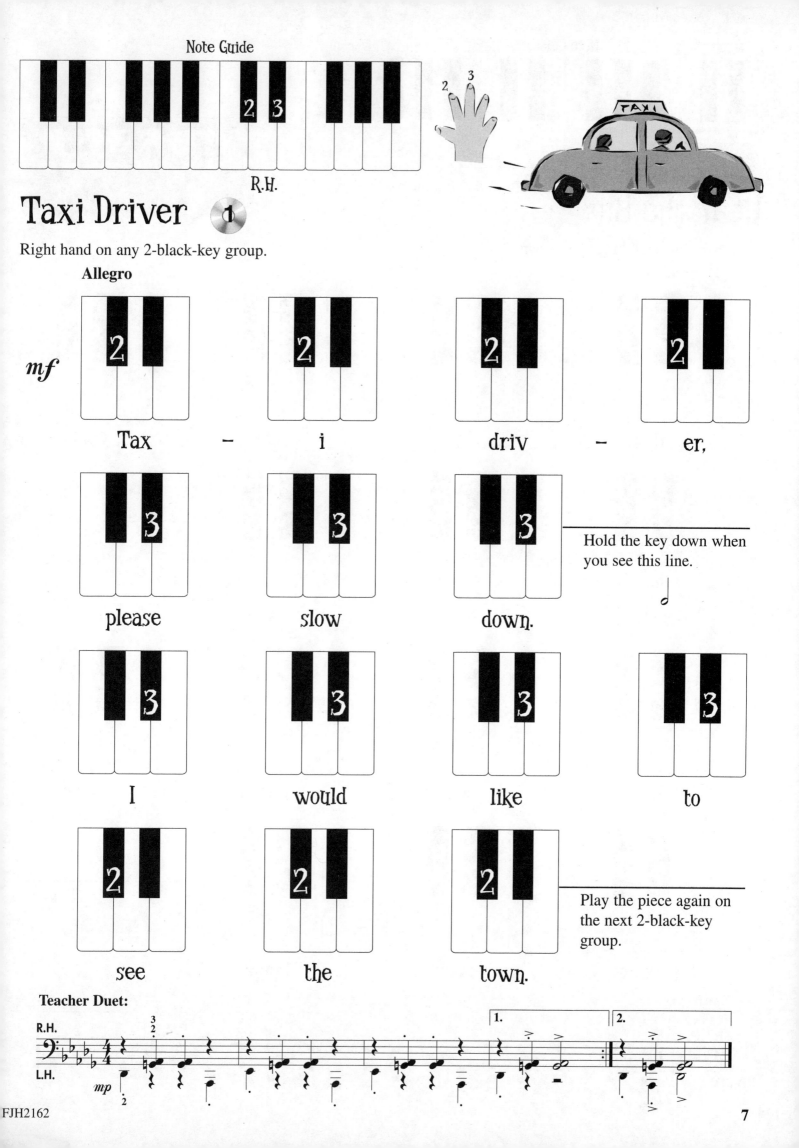

Note Guide

R.H.

Taxi Driver ①

Right hand on any 2-black-key group.

Allegro

mf

Tax – i driv – er,

please slow down.

Hold the key down when you see this line.

I would like to

see the town.

Play the piece again on the next 2-black-key group.

Teacher Duet:

R.H.

L.H.

mp

Note Guide

Hear the Bus 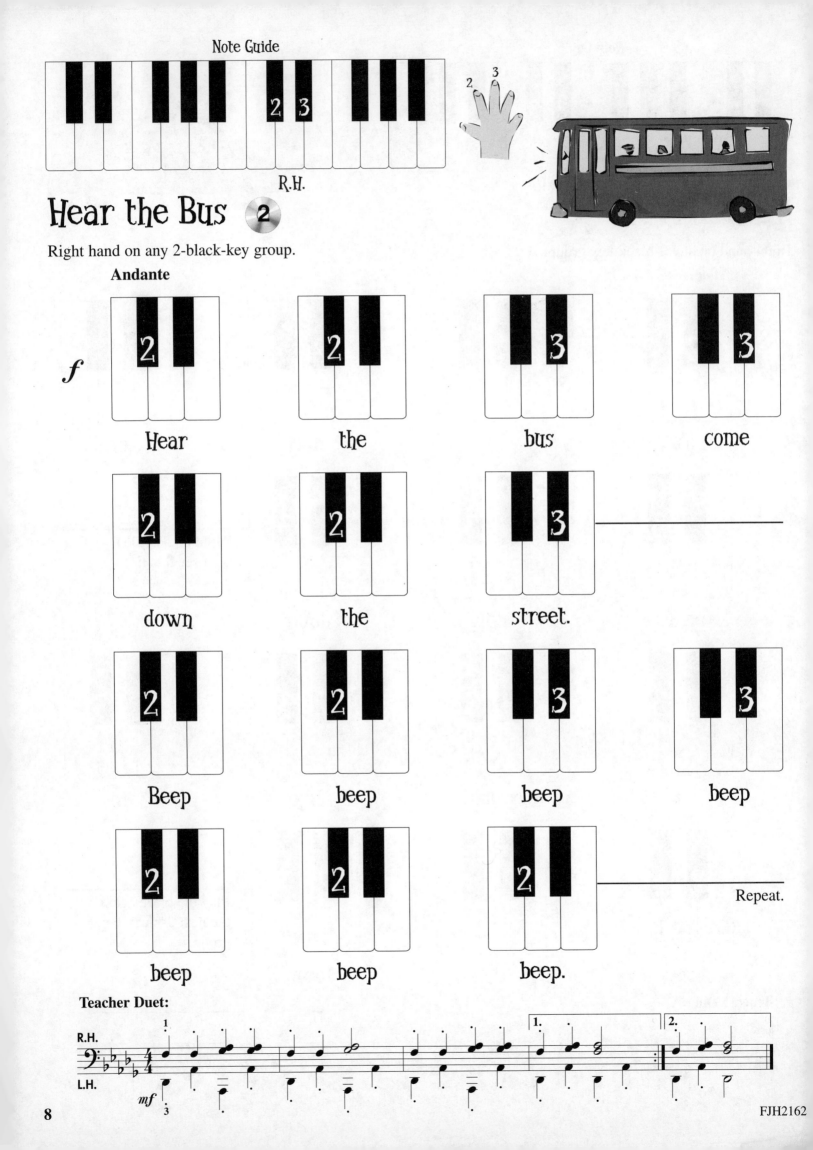 2

R.H.

Right hand on any 2-black-key group.

Andante

f

Hear

the

bus

come

down

the

street.

Beep

beep

beep

beep

beep

beep

beep.

Repeat.

Teacher Duet:

R.H.

L.H.

mf

FJH2162

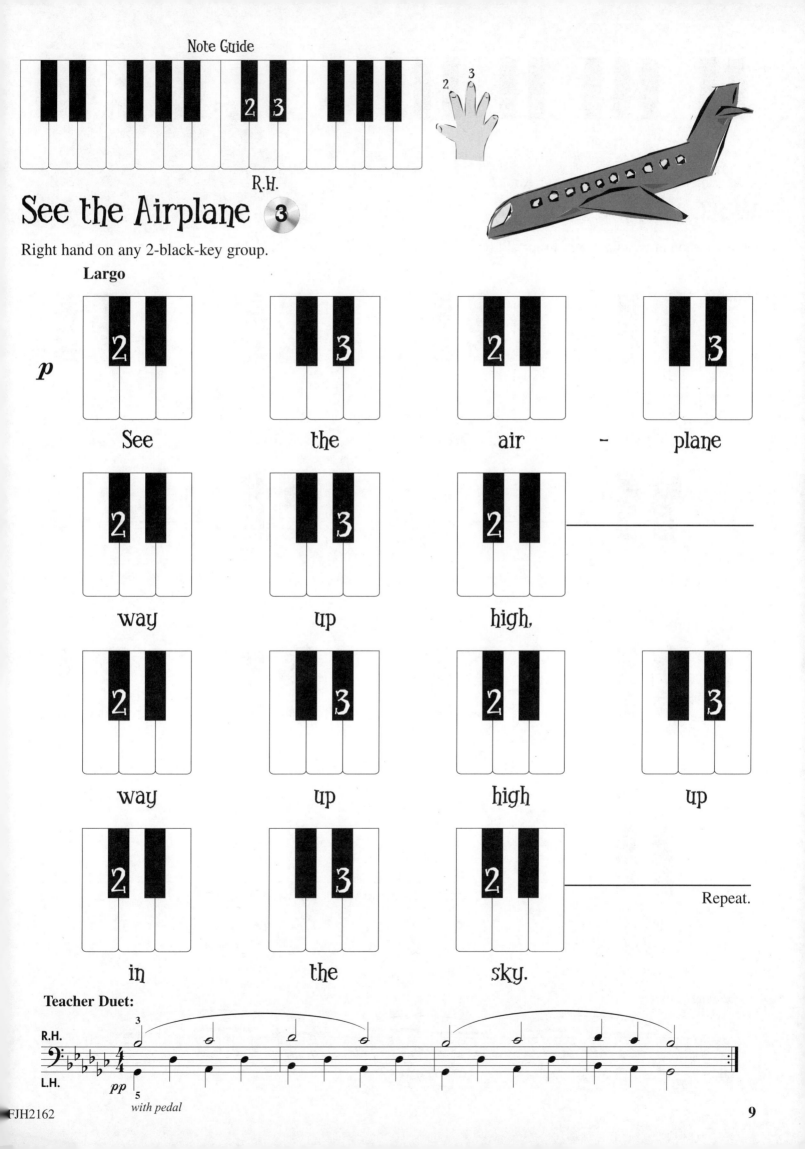

See the Airplane

Right hand on any 2-black-key group.

Teacher Duet:

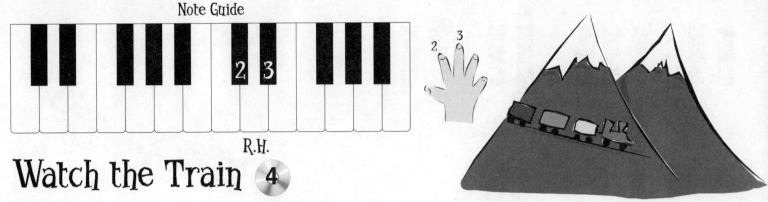

Note Guide

Watch the Train R.H. 4

Right hand on any 2-black-key group. Play both black keys at the same time when you see finger numbers 2 and 3 together.

Andante

mf

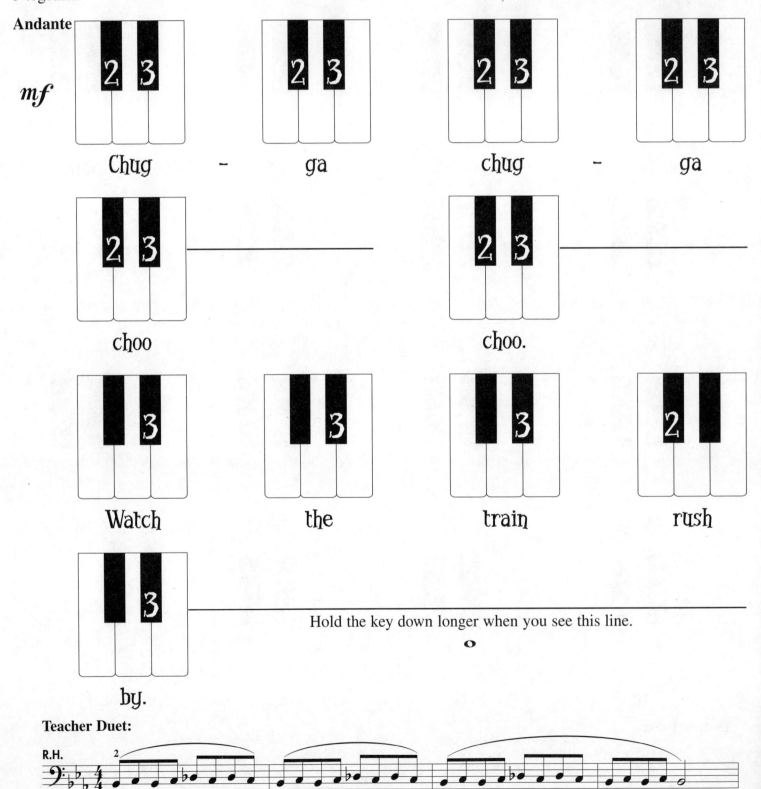

Chug – ga chug – ga

choo choo.

Watch the train rush

by.

Hold the key down longer when you see this line.

Teacher Duet:

R.H.

L.H. *mp*

FJH2162

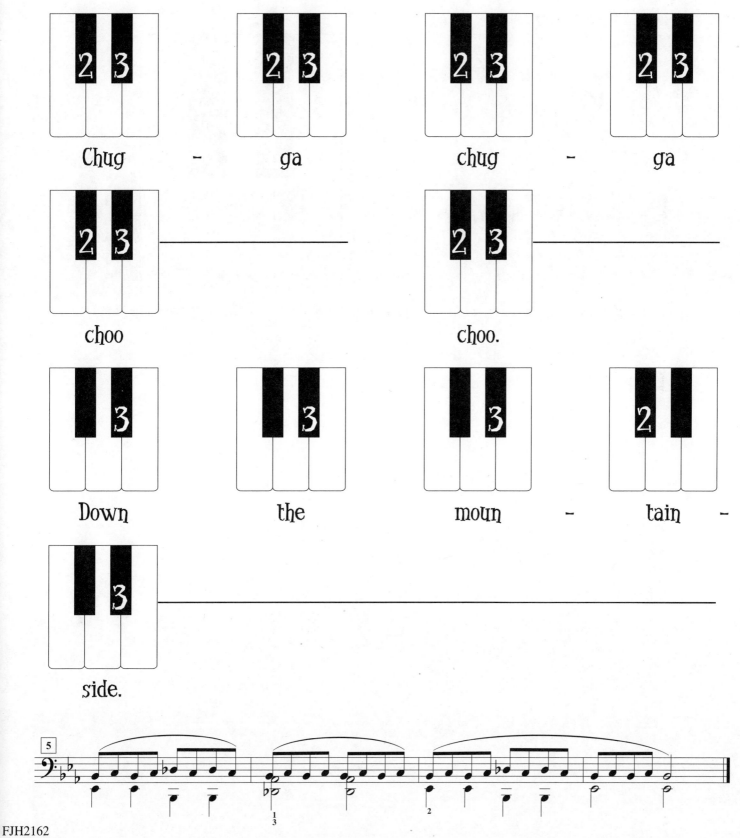

UNIT 2

 **Rug Time**

Sit on the floor and sing through the songs in the
Theory Made FUN Sing-Along Book tracks 1-11.

Visit **www.PianoMadeFun.com** for fun ideas to go along with this unit.

 **Piano Time**

Left Hand on the 2-Black-Key Group

Place your left hand fingers numbers 3 and 2 on any 2-black-key group on your piano.
Try playing them with nicely curved "spider fingers."

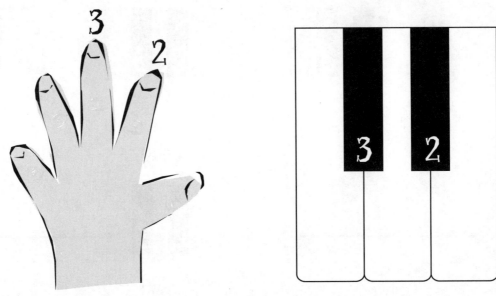

Have your teacher trace your left hand in the space below. Then write in 3 and 2 for the correct finger.

FJH2162

Note Guide

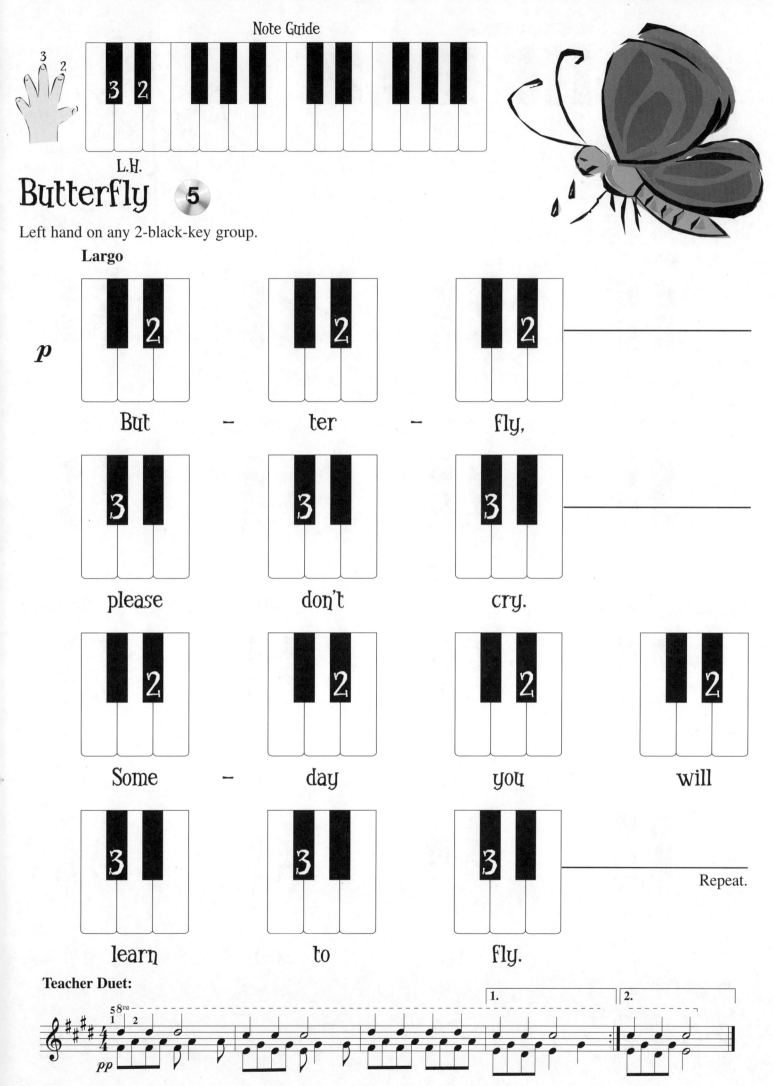

L.H.

Butterfly ⑤

Left hand on any 2-black-key group.

Largo

p

But – ter – fly,

please don't cry.

Some – day you will

learn to fly.

Repeat.

Teacher Duet:

Note Guide

So Hairy 6

Left hand on any 2-black-key group.

Andante

_f_

Spi   –   der,   spi   –   der,

he's   so   hair   –   y.

Do   you   think   that

he   is   scar   –   y?   Repeat.

Teacher Duet:

14   FJH2162

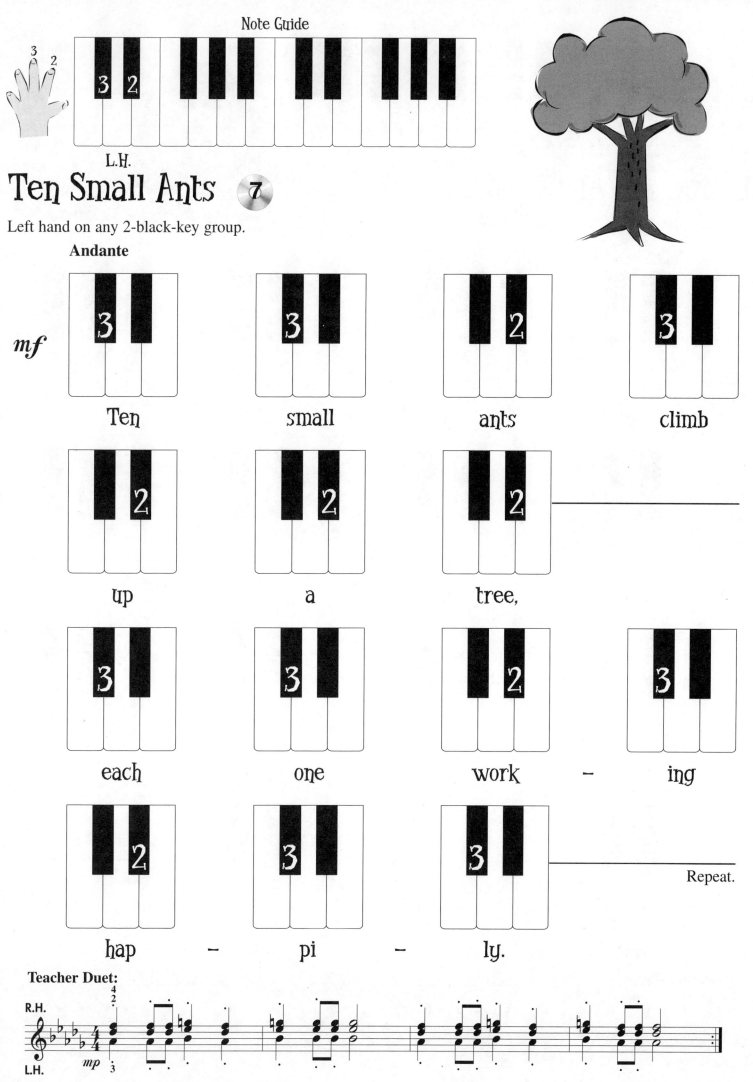

Ten Small Ants

Left hand on any 2-black-key group.

Andante

Ten	small	ants	climb
up	a	tree,	
each	one	work –	ing
hap –	pi –	ly.	Repeat.

Teacher Duet:

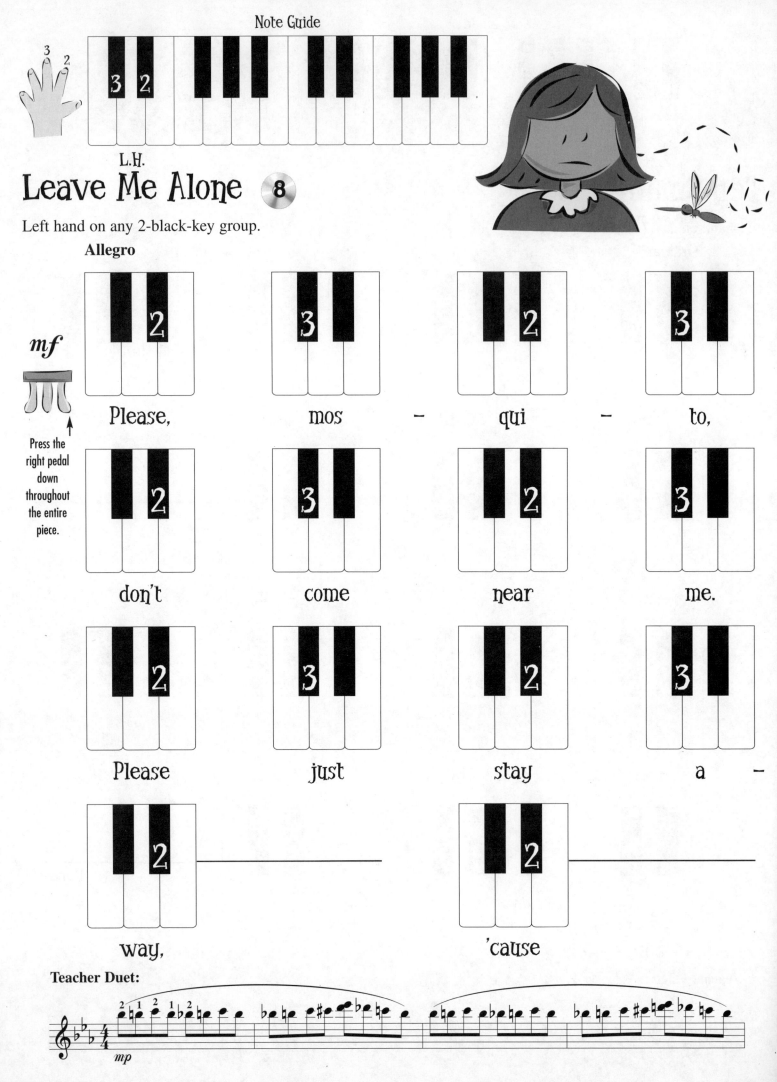

FJH2162

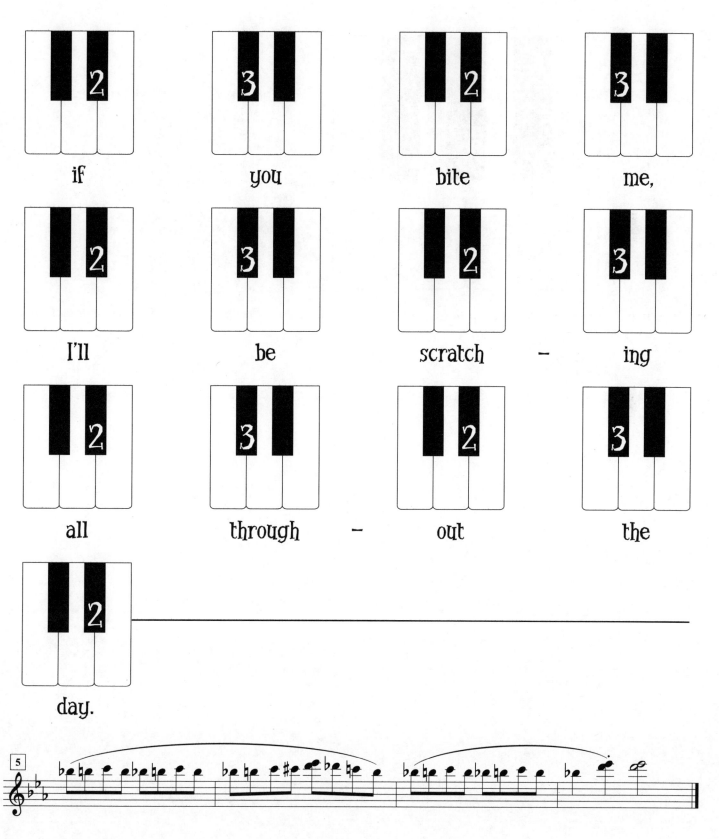

UNIT 3

 **Rug Time**

Sit on the floor and sing through the songs in the
Theory Made FUN Sing-Along Book tracks 1-11.

Visit **www.PianoMadeFun.com** for fun ideas to go along with this unit.

Piano Time

Right Hand on the 3-Black-Key Group

Place your right hand fingers 2, 3, and 4 on any 3-black-key group on your piano.
Try playing them with nicely curved "spider fingers."

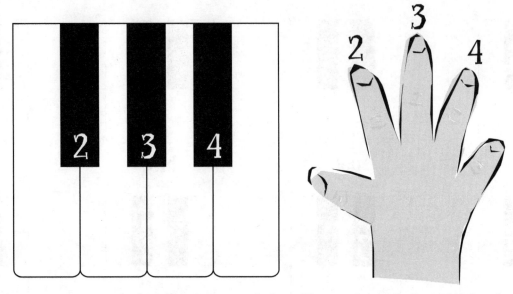

Have your teacher trace your right hand in the space below. Then write in 2, 3, and 4 for the correct fingers.

FJH2162

Note Guide

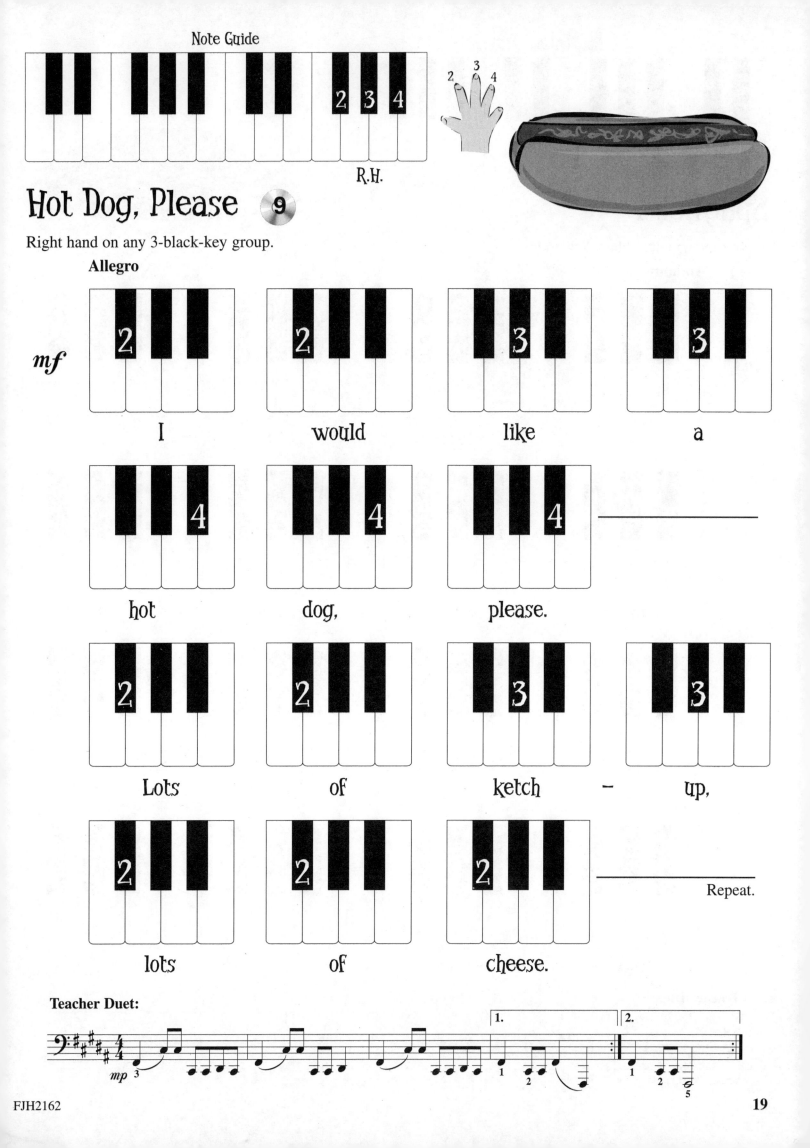

Hot Dog, Please

Right hand on any 3-black-key group.

Allegro

mf

I

would

like

a

hot

dog,

please.

Lots

of

ketch –

up,

lots

of

cheese.

Repeat.

Teacher Duet:

mp

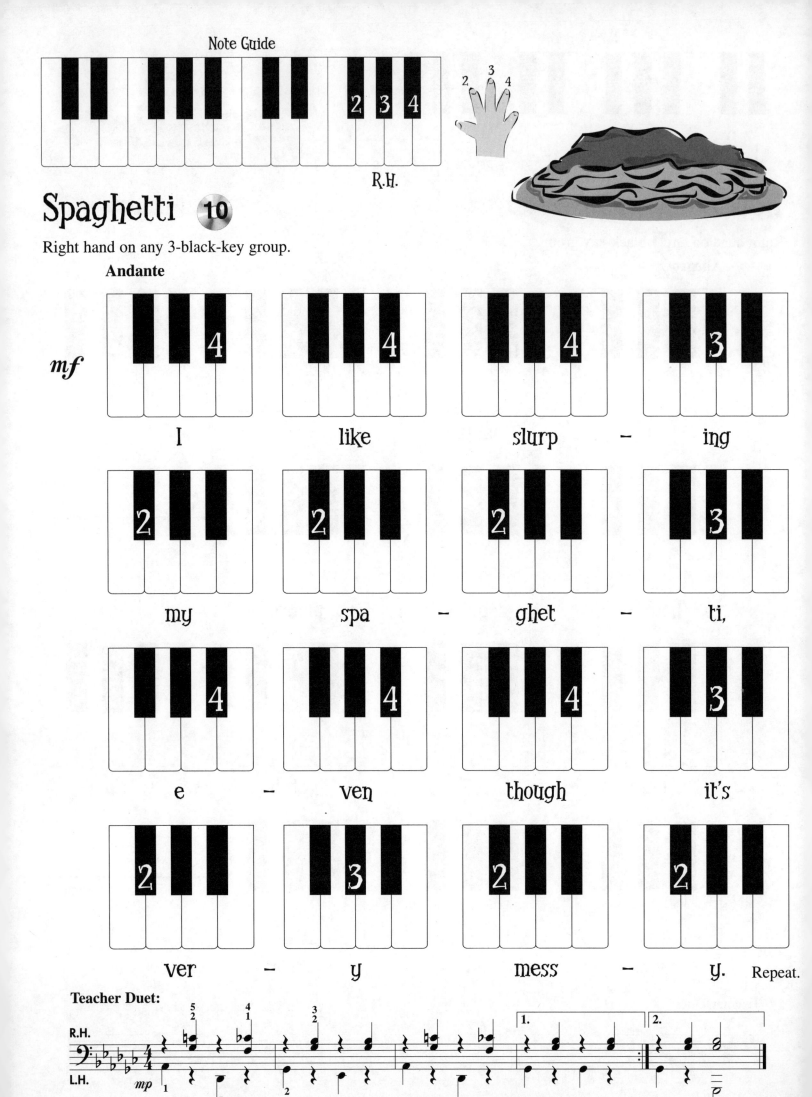

Spaghetti

Right hand on any 3-black-key group.

Andante

Teacher Duet:

FJH2162

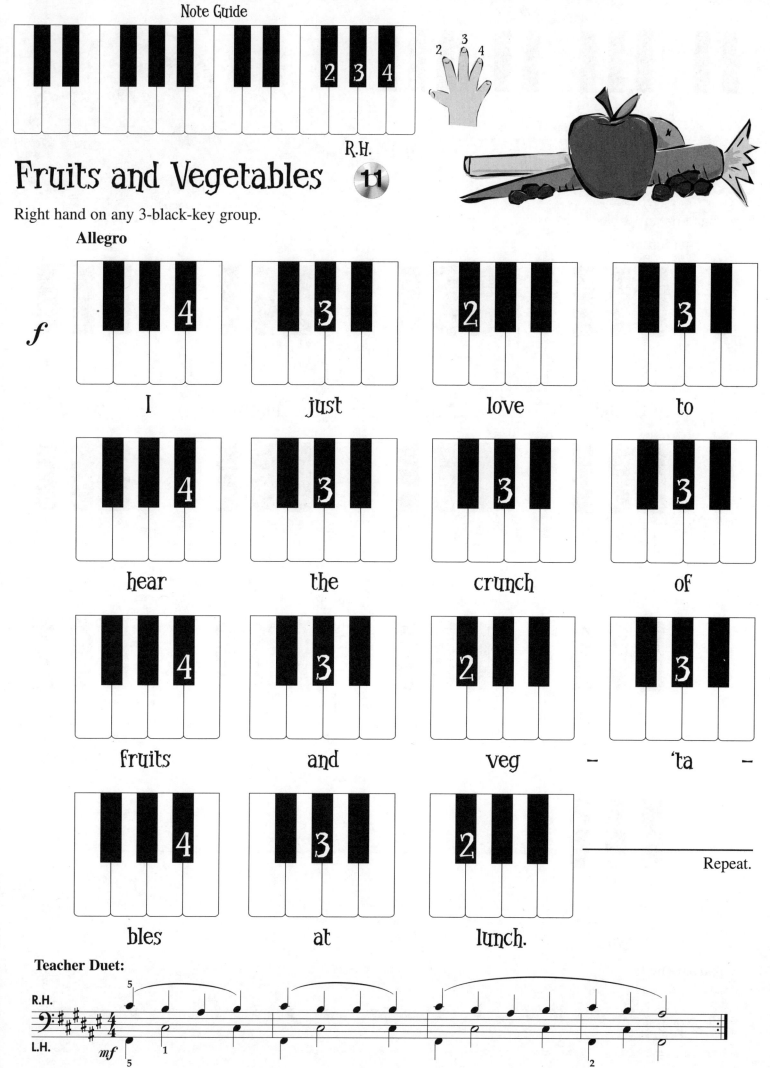

Note Guide

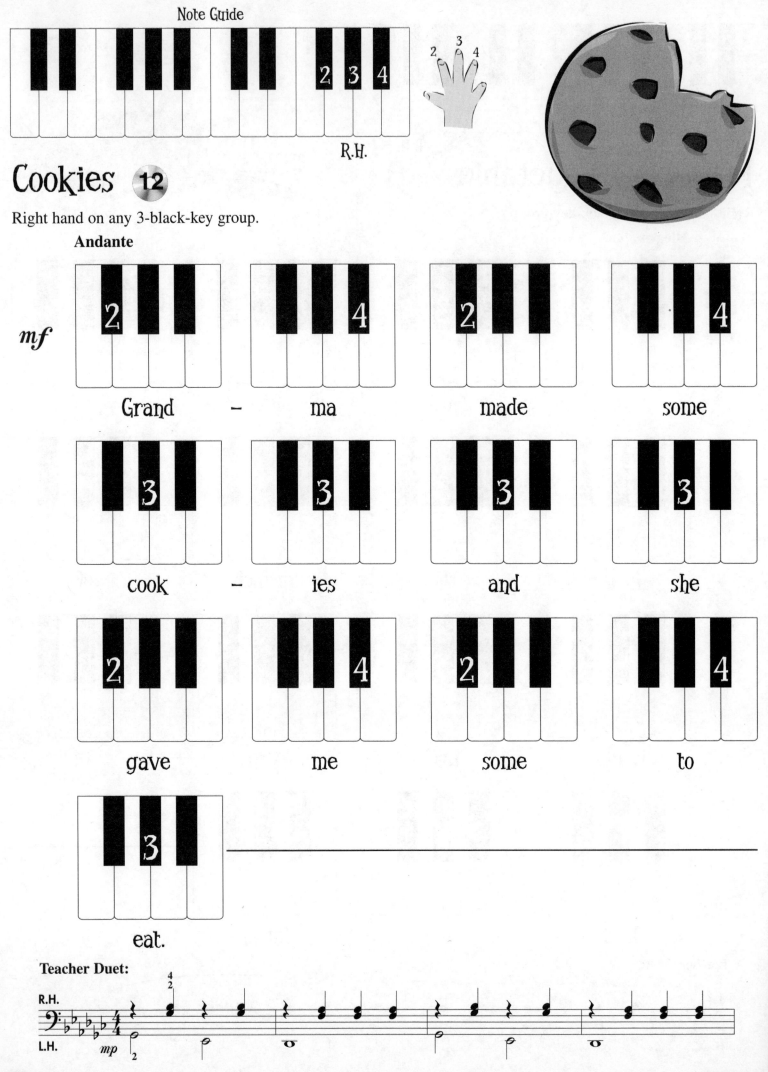

R.H.

Cookies 🔘12

Right hand on any 3-black-key group.

Andante

mf

Grand – ma made some

cook – ies and she

gave me some to

eat.

Teacher Duet:

FJH2162

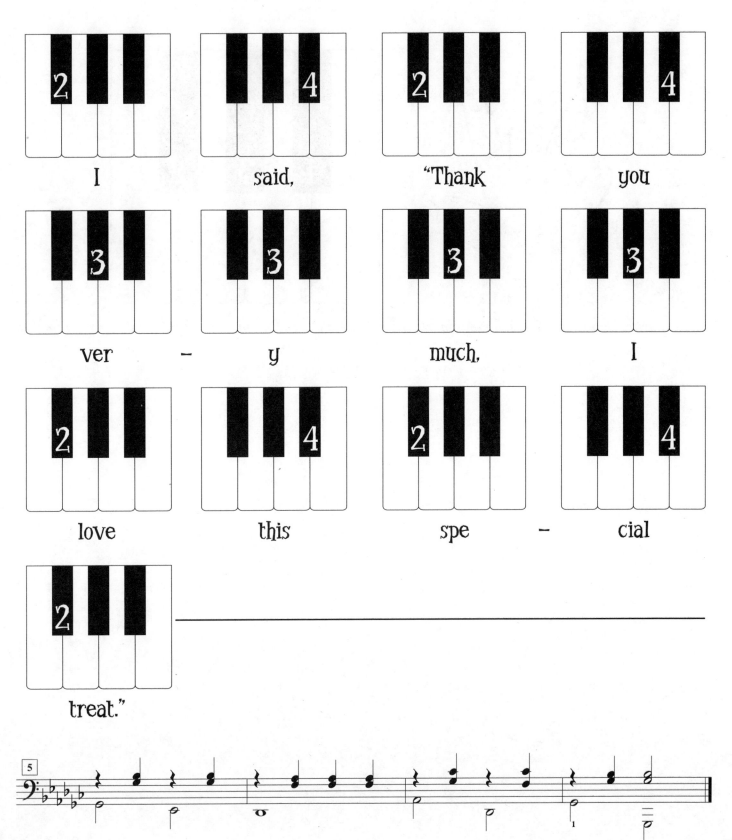

UNIT 4

 Rug Time

Sit on the floor and sing through the songs in the
Theory Made FUN Sing-Along Book track #'s 1-11.

Visit **www.PianoMadeFun.com** for fun ideas to go along with this unit.

 Piano Time

Left Hand on the 3-Black-Key Group

Place your left hand fingers 4, 3, and 2 on any 3-black-key group on your piano.
Try playing them with nicely curved "spider fingers."

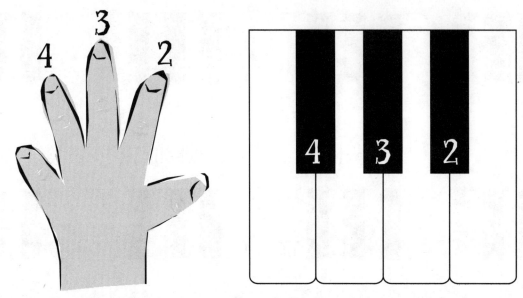

Have your teacher trace your left hand in the space below. Then write in 4, 3, and 2 for the correct fingers.

FJH2162

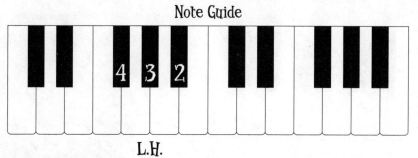

L.H.

Monkey, Monkey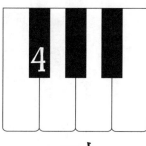

Left hand on any 3-black-key group.

Allegro

mf

 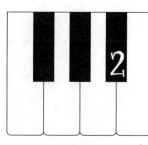 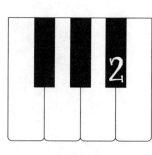 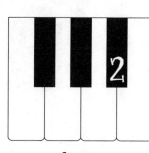

Mon – key,   mon – key,

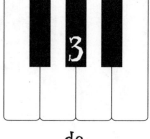  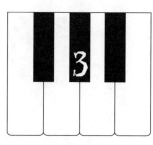

do   your   thing.

 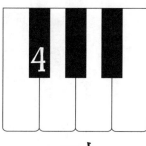  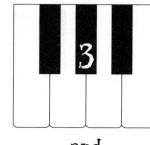

Play   and   run   and

  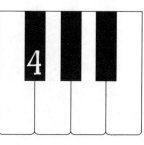

swing   and   swing.

Repeat.

Teacher Duet:

R.H.

L.H.   *mp*

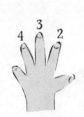
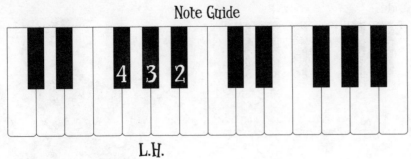

L.H.

Lazy Lion  14

Left hand on any 3-black-key group.

Largo

p

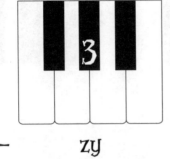  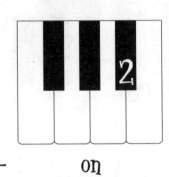

La – zy   li – on

sleeps   all   day;   He

 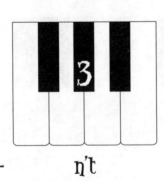 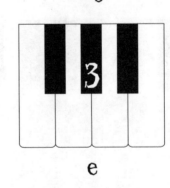 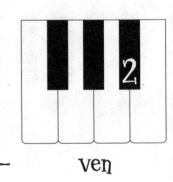

does – n't   e – ven

Repeat.

want   to   play.

Teacher Duet:

FJH2162

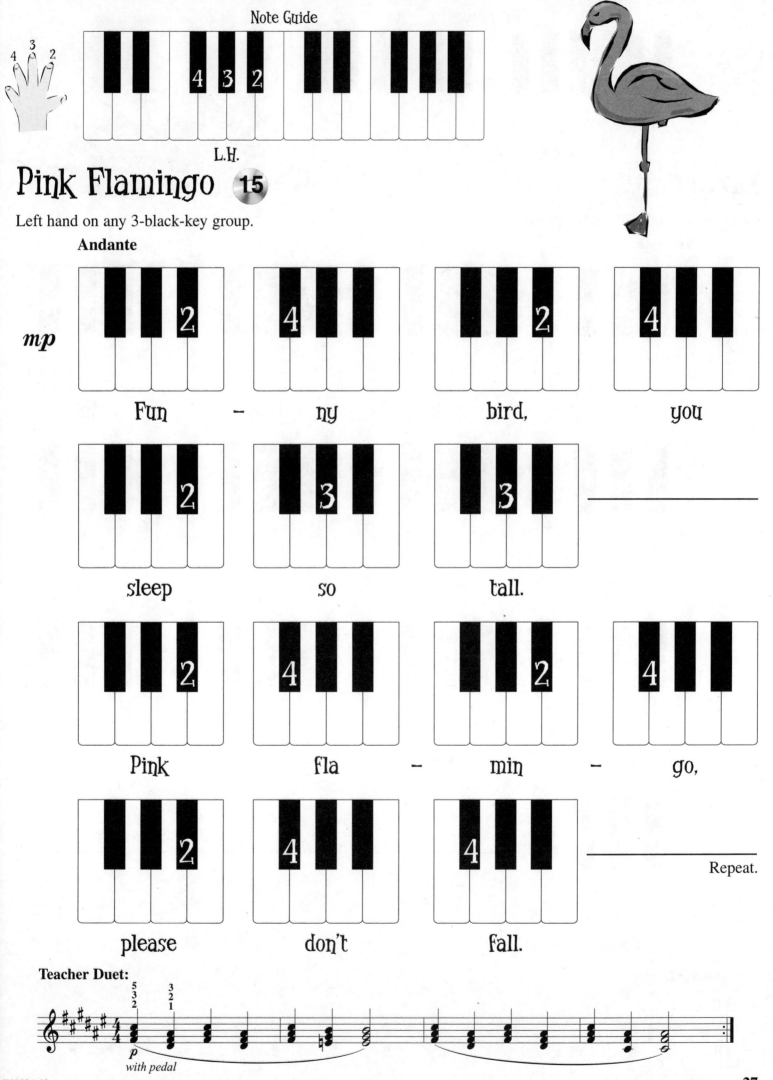

Note Guide

Pink Flamingo

L.H. 15

Left hand on any 3-black-key group.

Andante

mp

Fun – ny bird, you

sleep so tall.

Pink fla – min – go,

please don't fall.

Teacher Duet:

p
with pedal

Note Guide

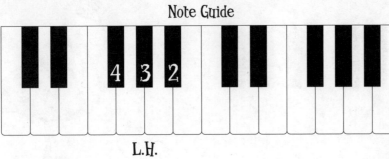

L.H.

Lizard 16

Left hand on any 3-black-key group.

Andante

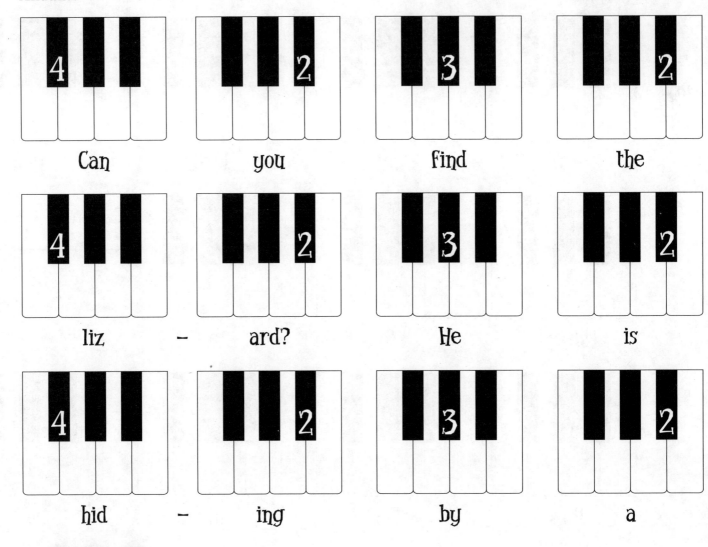

mf

Can   you   find   the

liz   –   ard?   He   is

hid   –   ing   by   a

rock.

Teacher Duet:

28

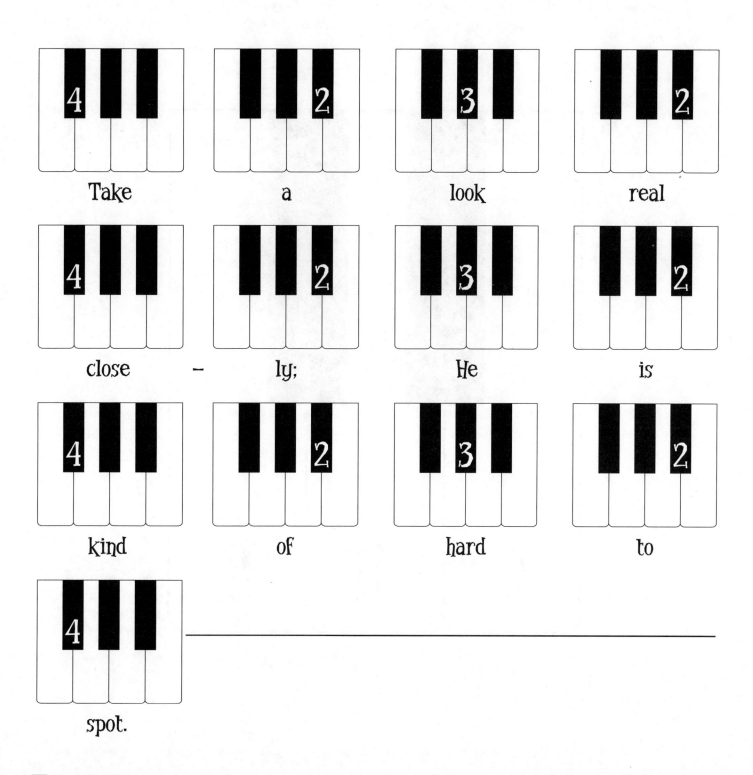

UNIT 5

 Rug Time

Sit on the floor and sing through the songs in the Theory Made FUN Sing-Along Book tracks 1 and 12-14.

Visit **www.PianoMadeFun.com** for fun ideas to go along with this unit.

 Piano Time

C, D, and E on the Piano Keyboard

In this unit, we will focus on C, D, and E on the piano keyboard. Remember to look for the 2-black-key groups first, since this will always help you find the white keys. *Play and name every C, D, and E on your piano keyboard. Your teacher will help you.*

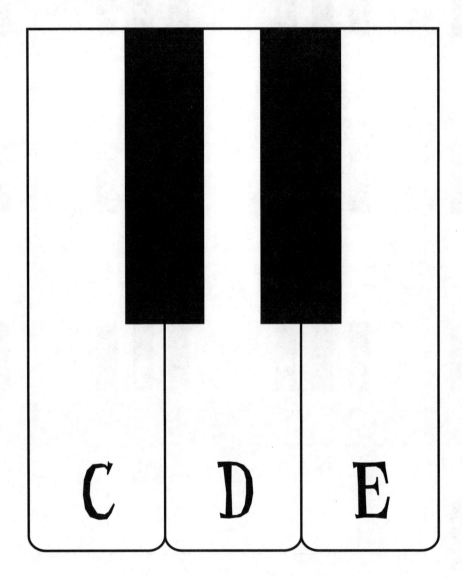

FJH2162

Trace the white key names on each of the keyboards below.

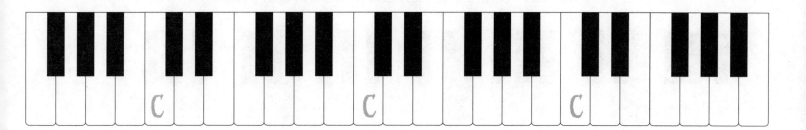

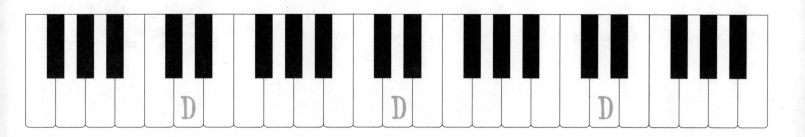

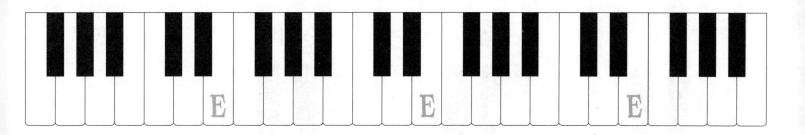

The pieces in the next two units will help you find, name, and play the white keys. For each new note, you will be playing an improv piece. You can play the new note in **any** octave and with **any** rhythm pattern that you want, as long as it matches the beat of the song. You can start by playing just one note at a time with a very simple rhythm. When you are comfortable, you can start playing more than one octave at a time, as well as changing the rhythm patterns. Your teacher can give you some ideas if you need them.

To the left of each 2-black-key group, you will always find C.

Two Black Keys, then C, C, C 17

Start with right hand on the 2-black-key group above Middle C, then repeat on each higher octave.

Andante

	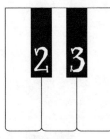	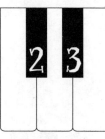	
Two	black	keys,	then
			Move up to the next octave and repeat.
C,	C,	C.	

Teacher Duet:

Play 4 times.

FJH2162

Cuckoo Clock Rock 18
(Improv on C)

Following the beat, play any of the C's on your piano. (Use R.H., L.H., or both.) Be creative and try different rhythms. Try making up words that fit the rhythms and match the title. Your teacher will show you how.

Allegro

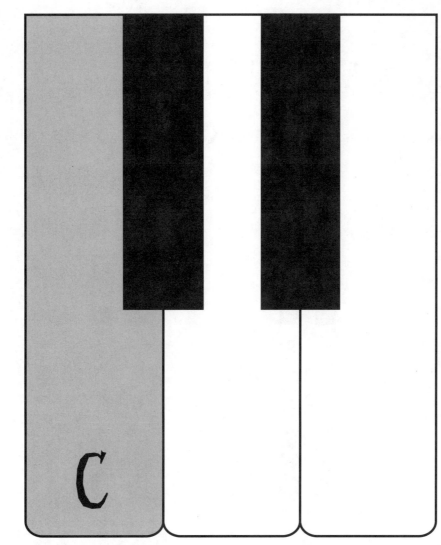

Color all of the C's below.

Teacher Duet:

Between each 2-black-key group, you will always find D.

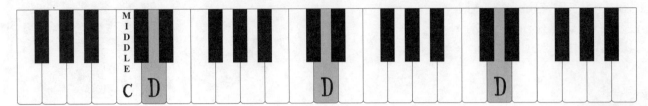

Two Black Keys, then D, D, D 19

Start with right hand on the 2-black-key group above Middle C, then repeat on each higher octave.

Andante

mf

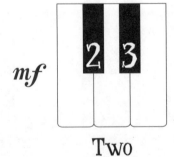

Two

black

keys,

then

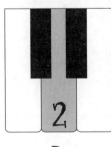

D,

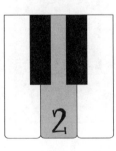

D,

D.

Move up to the next octave and repeat.

Teacher Duet:

Play 4 times.

R.H.

L.H.

mp

Dancing Drummer 20
(Improv on D)

Following the beat, play any of the D's on your piano. (Use R.H., L.H., or both.) Be creative and try different rhythms. Try making up words that fit the rhythms and match the title. Your teacher will show you how.

Allegro

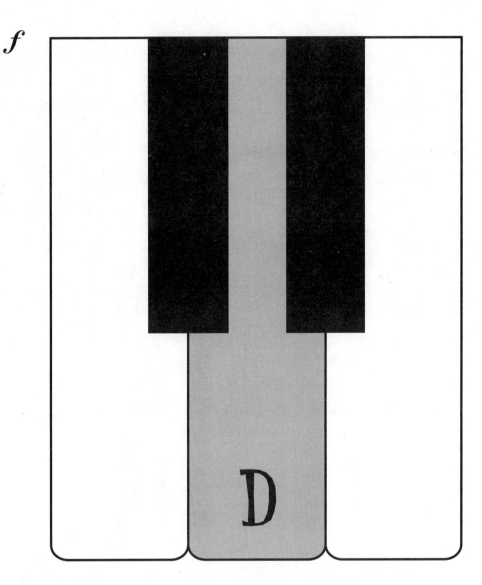

Color all of the D's below.

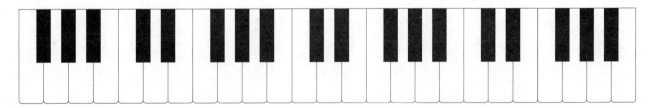

Teacher Duet:

To the right of each 2-black-key group, you will always find E.

Two Black Keys, then E, E, E

Start with right hand on the 2-black-key group above Middle C, then repeat on each higher octave.

Andante

mf

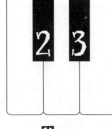

Two

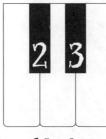

black

keys,

then

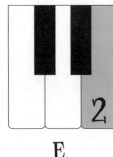

E,

E,

E.

Move up to
the next octave
and repeat.

Teacher Duet:

Eerie Evening
(Improv on E)

Following the beat, play any of the E's on your piano. (Use R.H., L.H., or both.) Be creative and try different rhythms. Try making up words that fit the rhythms and match the title. Your teacher will show you how.

Largo

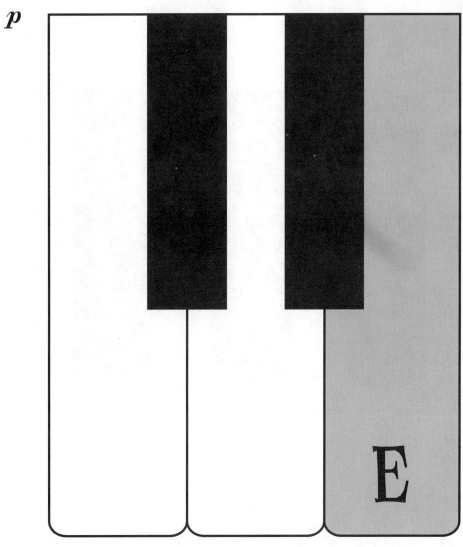

p

Color all of the E's below.

Teacher Duet:

UNIT 6

 Rug Time

Sit on the floor and sing through the songs in the Theory Made FUN Sing-Along Book tracks 1 and 12-14.

Visit **www.PianoMadeFun.com** for fun ideas to go along with this unit.

 Piano Time

F, G, A, and B on the Piano Keyboard

In this unit, we will focus on F, G, A, and B on the piano keyboard. Remember to look for the 3-black-key groups first, since this will always help you find the white keys. *Play and name every F, G, A, and B on your piano keyboard. Your teacher will help you.*

FJH2162

Trace the white key names on each of the keyboards below.

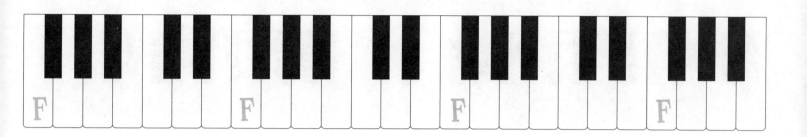

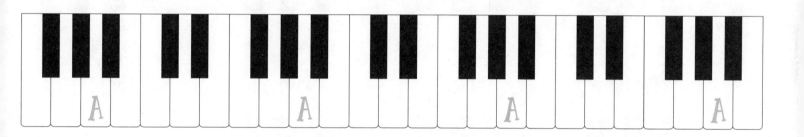

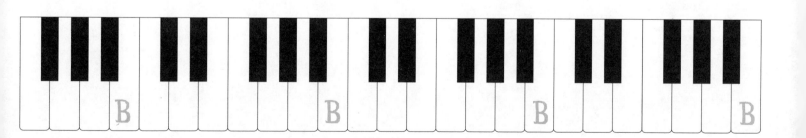

Practice the pieces in this unit the same way you did in Unit 5.

To the left of each 3-black-key group, you will always find F.

Three Black Keys, then F, F, F

Start with right hand on the 3-black-key group above Middle C, then repeat on each higher octave.

Andante

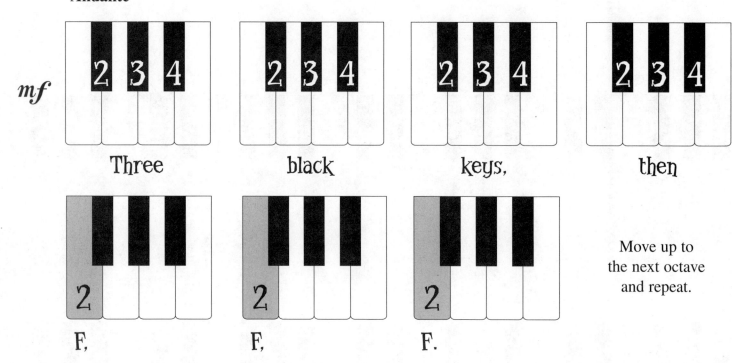

mf

Three   black   keys,   then

F,   F,   F.

Move up to
the next octave
and repeat.

Teacher Duet:

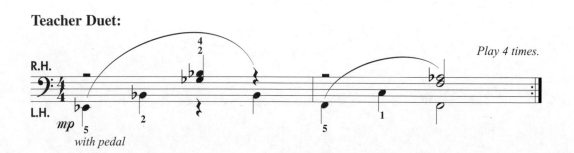

Play 4 times.

40

Fearless Fly 24
(Improv on F)

Following the beat, play any of the F's on your piano.
(Use R.H., L.H., or both.) Be creative and try different
rhythms. Try making up words that fit the rhythms
and match the title. Your teacher will show you how.

Andante

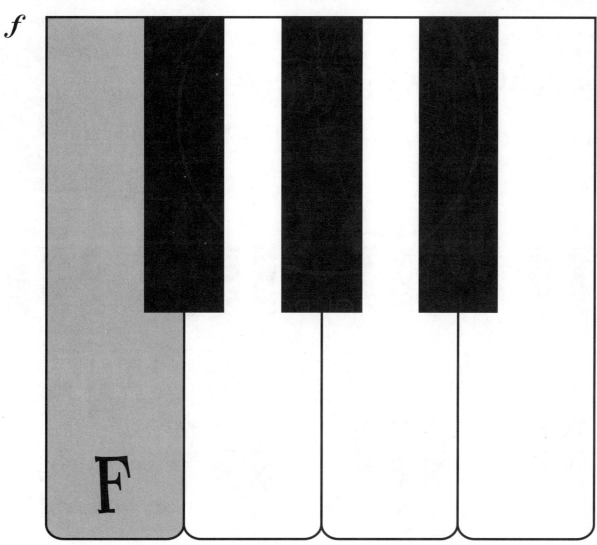

Color all of the F's below.

Teacher Duet:

Between the first and second black keys of each 3-black-key group, you will always find G.

Three Black Keys, then G, G, G

Start with right hand on the 3-black-key group above Middle C, then repeat on each higher octave.

Andante

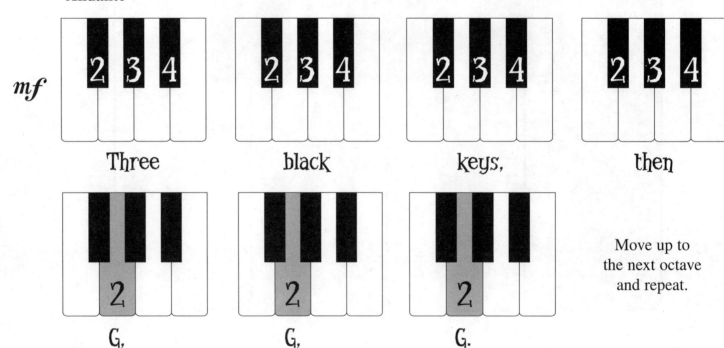

mf

Three   black   keys,   then

G,   G,   G.

Move up to the next octave and repeat.

Teacher Duet:

Play 4 times.

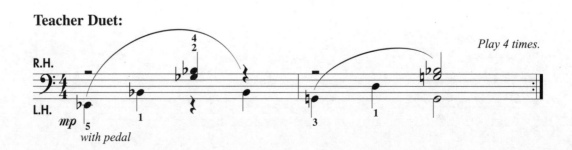

with pedal

Gentle Giant
(Improv on G)

Following the beat, play any of the G's on your piano. (Use R.H., L.H., or both.) Be creative and try different rhythms. Try making up words that fit the rhythms and match the title. Your teacher will show you how.

Largo

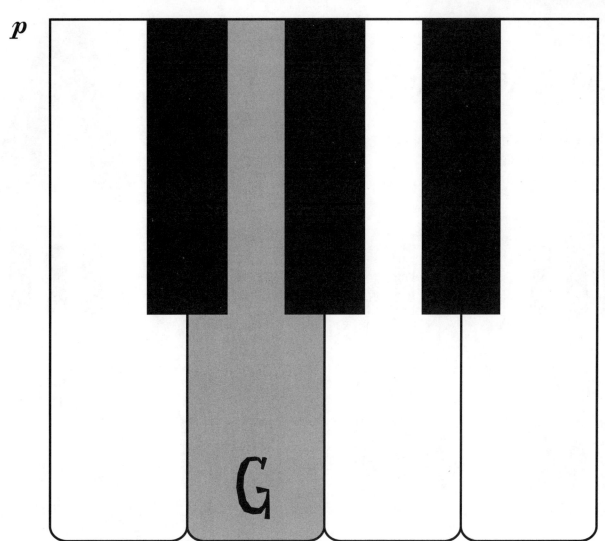

Color all of the G's below.

Teacher Duet:

Between the second and third black keys of each 3-black-key group, you will always find A.

Three Black Keys, then A, A, A

Start with right hand on the 3-black-key group above Middle C, then repeat on each higher octave.

Andante

mf

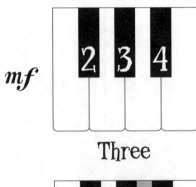
Three

black

keys,

then

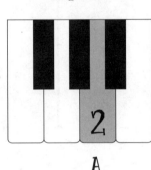
A,

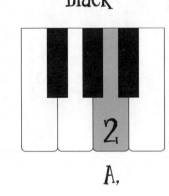
A,

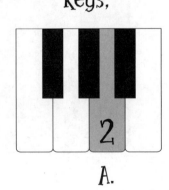
A.

Move up to the next octave and repeat.

Teacher Duet:

Play 4 times.

with pedal

Angry Agent
(Improv on A)

28

Following the beat, play any of the A's on your piano.
(Use R.H., L.H., or both.) Be creative and try different
rhythms. Try making up words that fit the rhythms
and match the title. Your teacher will show you how.

Andante

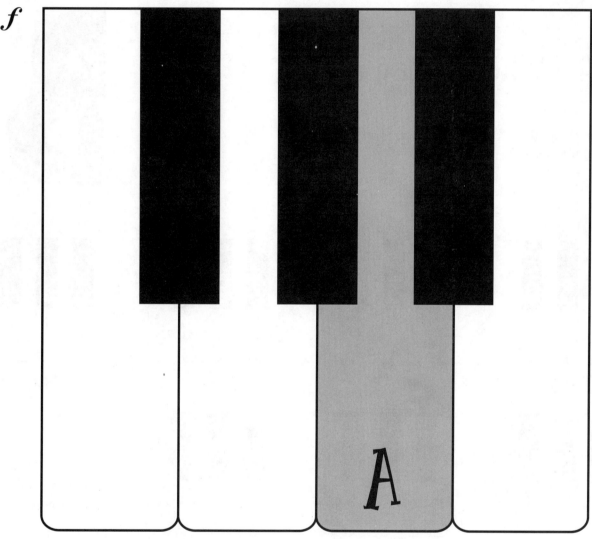

Color all of the A's below.

Teacher Duet:

To the right of each 3-black-key group, you will always find B.

Three Black Keys, then B, B, B  **29**

Start with right hand on the 3-black-key group above Middle C, then repeat on each higher octave.

Andante

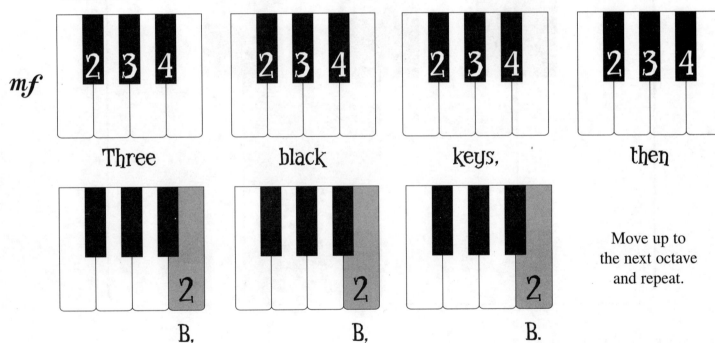

Teacher Duet:

Bouncing Bed Bugs 30
(Improv on B)

Following the beat, play any of the B's on your piano. (Use R.H., L.H., or both.) Be creative and try different rhythms. Try making up words that fit the rhythms and match the title. Your teacher will show you how.

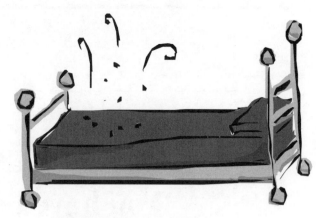

Andante

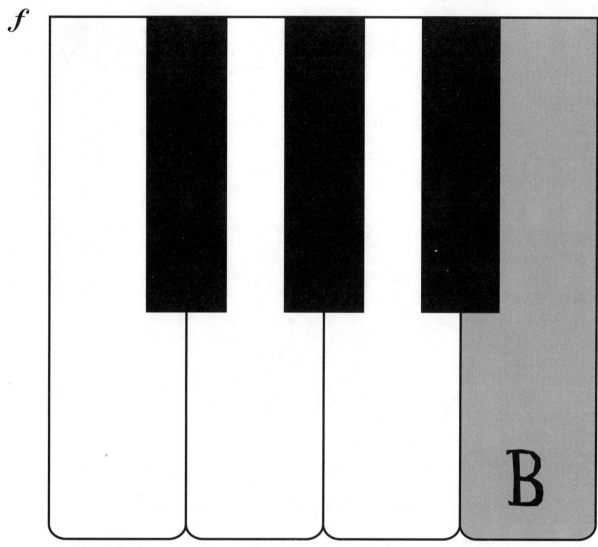

Color all of the B's below.

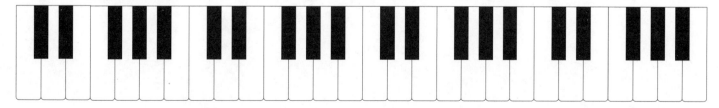

Teacher Duet:

Congratulations!
You have now completed the

Pre-Reading Made FUN
Starter Book

You are now ready to move on to

Note Reading Made FUN
Book 1

THE
F·J·H
MUSIC
COMPANY
INC.

Frank J. Hackinson